AF483767

ESSSENCE OF ALL RELIGIONS

NILESH KUMAR AGARWAL

This book, "The Essence of All Religions," is dedicated to all those people who give equal respect to all religions. Those who have been created by God believe in this world that God resides somewhere in every human being. This book will act as a guide for all those who have not learned to respect all religions in their lives. I hope that this book will be helpful to some extent in improving everyone's mindset and answering questions regarding different religions.

Thank you!

Contents

Foreword

Today, In modern times, people are interested in reading more fictional stories. Mr. Nilesh Kumar Agarwal is now ranked among the top ten mythological authors after Dr. Devdutt Pattanaik, Kavita Kane, Chitra Banerjee Divakaruni, Amish Tripathi, Ashwin Sanghi, and many others who have done a tremendous job in enlightening society with a mythological twist. These writers are better known for spreading awareness about Indian cultures and traditions in society.

Born in Meerut on December 25, 1989, Nilesh Kumar Agarwal grew up in Meerut, Uttar Pradesh. He completed his schooling at C.J.D.A.V. Public School, Meerut, and graduated from MAISM, Jaipur. His famous book "Indian Traditions and Their Scientific Reasons," which sold over 80,000 copies within just one year, helped him rank among the top ten mythological authors in India. He has also written many other books like Shiva Vaani, Krishna Vaani, Shree Ganesh, and Shiv-Krishna-Hanuman-Ganeshji Ke Updesh.

His podcast for Shiva Vaani has crossed more than 100,000 views on all platforms, including Spotify, Google Podcasts, Gaana, Jio Saavn, Wynk, Hungama, Hubhopper, and many others, within a month of its release. Mr. Nilesh Kumar Agarwal is also the founder of the NGO "Nilesh Staallion Foundation," a crowdfunding platform that provides medical assistance to all living beings and funds environmentally friendly start-up projects.

All his books are written in a very simple language, whether they're in English or Hindi. You can easily find all his books on Amazon.com, Flipkart.com, NotionPress.com, and all other leading platforms.

Preface

When a human being is born into this world, he does not know anything. Whatever his parents, relatives, friends, teachers, etc. teach him, that knowledge gives him the direction to live his life. But how can it be decided how much of that knowledge is right and how much is wrong? It is decided by the Scriptures, which were composed by God. It doesn't matter which religion you choose. Because no religion teaches us to fight, quarrel, or hurt anyone. But man gets his knowledge from people, from those who may not have read or understood those texts properly. That is why, if you want to understand life, read your scriptures yourself and try to understand what God wants to say to you. It will be as if there are no rules to any game in today's world. If you don't know the rules, will you be able to play that game properly? No.

Now the question comes of which scripture we should read or which religion we should accept. The answer is that you should read all the scriptures and understand all the religions. Just as the way to reach a destination may be different, everyone's destination is the same. Every religion teaches liberty, equality, and fraternity. Every religion says that whatever religion in this world you follow, just make sure the deeds are good. God is a tree, whose different branches have been given the form of religion. Every twig means that some leaves, i.e., people, come from every religion. But every branch forgets that its root is the same, and its leaves are also the same. A person who understands this always achieves success in life. This is the reason that only a few people are successful in the world: they have complete knowledge of their scriptures.

In this book, I have included some of the things that I have gotten from the Vedas, Puranas, Quran, Bible, and other religious texts. This book contains all that is common to all religions. This, along with making every human being a better person, makes man aware of the rules of this world.

Prologue

There are many such things in the Bhagavad Gita and the Bible of Jesus that are exactly the same. This is also because Buddha was born 623 years before Jesus was born, and the teachings he taught reached the Greek community even before Jesus was born. Enlightenment in Buddhism is reached through the Gita. Gautam Buddha followed the Gita and spread what he agreed upon as Buddhism to the rest of the world.

Whatever the religion, there is only one God. Therefore, the things told by God are also the same. Gautam Buddha was a great thinker, and he spread the message of God in the world through his intuition.

The teachings given in the Bhagavad Gita, Bible, and Quran are related to spirituality, not religion. But today's man in this world sees and understands all these teachings from the religious point of view instead of understanding them from the spiritual point of view. One has to awaken himself to the state of self-knowledge and understand that God is not attained by following religion but by following spirituality.

Now let me introduce you to some similarities that are exactly the same in the Gita and the Bible.

In the seventh chapter of the Bhagavad Gita, Shri Krishna says that all the intelligent people who are there all love me, and I love them. Similarly, in the Bible, it is said by Jesus (John XIV. 21) that the one who loves me will be loved by both me and my Father.

In the ninth chapter of the Bhagavad Gita, Shri Krishna says that he is the guide, supporter, master, abode, refuge, and friend of humans. Similarly, in the Bible, it is said by Jesus (John XIV. 6) that He is the way of life for humans and the truth. I am the beginning of man, and I am the end.

In the sixth chapter of the Bhagavad Gita, Shri Krishna says that nothing in this world can ever be separated from me, and neither can I be separated from them. Similarly, in the Bible, it is said by Jesus (John VI. 57) that the whole world resides in me and I reside in the whole world.

It is also said by Shri Krishna in the sixth chapter of the Bhagavad Gita that those who worship me with true devotion and love always reside in me, and I in them. Similarly, in the Bible, it is said by Jesus (John XVII:23) that I can be perfected in humans and humans in myself.

In the ninth chapter of the Bhagavad Gita, it has also been said by Shri Krishna that a person who worships me with true devotion never faces any calamity. Similarly, it is said by Jesus in the Bible (John 3:5, NIV) that whoever believes in me will never be punished and live a happy life.

In the tenth chapter of the Bhagavad Gita, Shri Krishna says that he is the beginning, middle, and end of all living entities and non-living things. Similarly, as said by Jesus in the Bible (Rev. I. 8), I am the beginning, middle, and end of all.

In the eighteenth chapter of the Bhagavad Gita, it has been said by Shri Krishna, "O man!" I will deliver you from all sins; why do you worry? Similarly, it is said by Jesus in the Bible (Matt. IX. 2) that "son," you'll be happy forever and all your sins will be forgiven.

In the ninth chapter of the Bhagavad Gita, Shri Krishna says that whatever sacrifice, charity, or penance is performed without faith is never fruitful and is inauspicious. Similarly, it is said by Jesus in the Bible (Rom. XIV. 23) that whatever is done without faith is tantamount to sin.

ONE
ESSENCE OF ALL RELIGIONS

Every religion says that a man's experiences definitely save him from wrong decisions, but his experiences come only from wrong decisions.

ᐯᐯᐯ

Every religion says that the most expensive thing in a man's life is peace.

ᐯᐯᐯ

Every religion says that any living being on this earth sheds tears only when there is a lot of pain in its heart.

ᐯᐯᐯ

Every religion says that the best friend in a man's life is his confidence.

ϷϷϷ

Every religion says that a man should understand, with the example of a needle, how he walks on the cloth and sews it, because it is not necessary that every prickly thing has a bad purpose.

ϷϷϷ

Every religion says that a man should keep in mind that he should not focus on someone calling him good, but try to focus on that person who calls him bad.

ϷϷϷ

Every religion says that in human life, man should remember that as long as he has faith in God, there will always be a way out of his every confusion.

ϷϷϷ

Every religion says that one should remember that if a sick person is to be cured, then cook khichdi in a vessel, because if you cook khichdi in the mind, it will make a person sick.

ϷϷϷ

Every religion says that one should always remain calm, no matter what one says, because no matter how strong the sun may be, it can never dry the sea.

ᗏᗏᗏ

Every religion says that in human life, a person can win or lose, but it is difficult to beat the one who wins the hearts of others.

ᗏᗏᗏ

Every religion says that if a man wants to reduce the difficulties in his life, then he has to understand the difference between his needs and desires.

ᗏᗏᗏ

Every religion says that in this world it is very difficult to defeat a person who has learned to walk by stumbling blocks.

ᗏᗏᗏ

Every religion says that the most valuable thing for a man in this world is sleep, peace, air, and breath. And he gets it for free, yet he doesn't appreciate it.

ᗏᗏᗏ

Every religion says that in this world there are certain things a man has to ignore in his life; if he knows this, then no one can stop him from being successful.

ϷϷϷ

Every religion says that in this world, the person who is not afraid of his future can only enjoy the best of his present.

ϷϷϷ

Every religion says that if a person in this world makes himself good instead of looking for good people, then perhaps the search for someone else will be completed by meeting him.

ϷϷϷ

Every religion says that only man in this world is young and keeps on learning, even if he is old. And every person who stops learning is old, even if he is young. A man should always keep his mind young in his life.

ϷϷϷ

Every religion says that the most difficult task for a man in this world is to assess himself; he should keep trying continuously to improve himself.

❦❦❦

Every religion says that if a man wants to be happy in this world, then he has to reduce his grievances. Otherwise, the more complaints there are, the more unhappy he will be.

❦❦❦

Every religion says that in human life one should not be proud of his fame because in his last days he needs someone's support.

❦❦❦

Every religion says that in human life it is very important to understand that the work obtained by recognition lasts only for a short time, but the identity obtained by work lasts for a lifetime.

❦❦❦

Every religion says that in this world, for a man, his upbringing and his rites are very important; just by reading and writing, one does not become a human.

❦❦❦

Every religion says that in the life of a man in this world, likewise, a person does not have to do bad deeds; they get done by him, and in the same way, good deeds are not done automatically; a man has to do it himself.

ⱷⱷⱷ

Every religion says that in this world, man can reach heights only by thinking of change; through vengeance, he only creates obstacles for himself.

ⱷⱷⱷ

Every religion says that one should remember that only certain desires are good, in which case there is no need to pledge self-respect.

ⱷⱷⱷ

Every religion says that one should believe that the decisions made by God are better than the wishes of every human being.

ⱷⱷⱷ

Every religion says that if a person wants to understand life, then he has to look back, i.e., in the past, and if he wants to live life, then he has to look forward, i.e., towards his future.

ᐅᐅᐅ

Every religion says that a person should keep this in mind in his life: that just as the winds change the course of the weather, prayers change the attitude of trouble.

ᐅᐅᐅ

Every religion says that a man should keep this in mind in his life: that the life he got is a matter of luck, his death is a matter of time, but even after death, it is a matter of deeds to remain alive in the hearts of people.

ᐅᐅᐅ

Every religion says that a man's life begins to end the day humans keep silent on the issues that matter to their lives.

ᐅᐅᐅ

Every religion says that one should be patient in life because the time comes for everyone. Just as the calendar always changes the date, one day such a date also comes, which changes the calendar itself.

ᐅᐅᐅ

Every religion says that in human life, even if the loud voice of a false person silences the true person, the silence of the true person always shakes the roots of the false person.

ᛈᛈᛈ

Every religion says that it is not wrong for a man to lose in the world, but it is wrong to give up.

ᛈᛈᛈ

Every religion says that human behavior should be like a needle and not like a scissor because the needle works to unite two and the scissor works to cut one into two.

ᛈᛈᛈ

Every religion says that one should always remember that as long as you have friends, so will your future; that is why one should choose friends wisely.

ᛈᛈᛈ

Every religion says that one should always remember not to misuse time because even time does not have enough time to give it to anyone again.

ɷɷɷ

Every religion says that if a person understands his own human life, then there is joy in his life alone, and if he does not understand, then he is all alone throughout his life.

ɷɷɷ

Every religion says that if a man speaks through his mind, then decisions are made, but if he keeps them in mind, then there are differences.

ɷɷɷ

Every religion says that man should learn to forgive because he himself expects this from his God.

ɷɷɷ

Every religion says that the relationship between human beings is not deepened by talking about big things but by understanding small feelings. The cost of a mirror may be less than a diamond, but after wearing diamond jewelry, everyone looks for a mirror only.

ϷϷϷ

Every religion says that in this world, man is defeated only when he stops walking, but time works in the opposite direction. Because whether it is sun or shade, black night or rain, no matter how bad the situation, time always goes on. That's why time wins; if a man also keeps on moving like time, he too will never lose.

ϷϷϷ

Every religion says that when time takes a turn in the life of any human being in this world, it not only turns the tides but also changes the whole life of that person.

ϷϷϷ

Every religion says that no man can be happy in this world unless it is more important in his life to look happy than to be happy.

ϷϷϷ

Every religion says that the best friend of a person in this world is his conscience, who praises good deeds and shakes him up on bad deeds.

ϷϷϷ

Every religion says that in this world it is necessary for a person to know what is most important to him in his life. If a man knows this, then he can achieve those things even in difficult situations.

ᗡᗡᗡ

Every religion says that man keeps on moving around in his life with a bundle of karma; that is how he fills it through his own deeds, and this is also the law of life.

ᗡᗡᗡ

Every religion says that if human beings are not excited about any goal as soon as they wake up in the morning, then that human being is not living, only taking life.

ᗡᗡᗡ

Every religion says that in this world, a man should remember that no matter how difficult he finds his life, he can always do something and be successful in it.

ᗡᗡᗡ

Every religion says that in this world man should always keep his eyes on what he wants to get, but man does the opposite; he keeps his eyes on what he has lost.

ᎠᎠᎠ

Every religion says that in this world, man should live his life according to the choice of God because in this world, people's choices and people themselves keep on changing.

ᎠᎠᎠ

Every religion says that in this world if a man fights for his life by making God a justice, then victory will always be his.

ᎠᎠᎠ

Every religion says that in this world, man should never give up hope in God and should never expect anything from the world.

ᎠᎠᎠ

Every religion says that after imagining a man in this world, he should also implement it; nothing will be achieved just by looking at the stairs until you climb them.

ᎠᎠᎠ

Every religion says that if a man wants peace in this world, he can only get it through himself; others will only get entangled.

༻༺༻

Every religion says that in this world if a person should give these three gifts i.e. helping someone along with time and dedication, then he should never leave the company of such a person.

༻༺༻

Every religion says that every task in this world is difficult for every human being before it becomes easy for them.

༻༺༻

Every religion says that in this world, man should remember that he should never pretend that he has no shortage of time.

༻༺༻

Every religion says that in this world, a man may regret his speech, but he will never regret his silence.

༻༺༻

Every religion says that in this world only friendship can double man's happiness and ease half his sorrows.

᠊᠊᠊

Every religion says that if a person takes a lamp for others in this world, then the light will fall on him too and his face will also shine.

᠊᠊᠊

Every religion says that in this world where man's virtues uplift him, his sins snatch everything from him by slapping him.

᠊᠊᠊

Every religion says that in this world, men should remember that if a lion sits on a rock, that rock is also called a throne. Therefore, try to become a lion, not to get the throne, so wherever you sit, that place becomes your throne.

᠊᠊᠊

Every religion says that if a person in this world has a tendency to get a stone with his name printed or to get his name printed by giving a little donation, then he comes in the low category because it does not give charity or service but to get praised. The sense of ego is hidden in this kind of work.

ﭘﭘﭘ

Every religion says that in this world, if a person starts considering dust as a color in the journey of his life, then it reflects that he has started understanding every move of his life.

ﭘﭘﭘ

Every religion says that in this world, one human crosses the path of another, and cats are just as infamous for crossing paths with humans.

ﭘﭘﭘ

Every religion says that if a man does not set rules for himself in this world, then he has to follow the rules made by others.

ﭘﭘﭘ

Every religion says that if any person in this world needs your advice, then give your advice along with your assistance because the advice might go wrong, but not the assistance.

ﭘﭘﭘ

Every religion says that man should remember that as long as he is immersed in his ego, he will neither see his own faults nor the goodness of others.

ᚦᚦᚦ

Every religion says that even if a human being does not speak, then his words can only be listened to by God. But if God does not speak and yet a man listens, then he is a true devotee.

ᚦᚦᚦ

Every religion says that in this human life, a man may forgive someone again and again, but a man should believe in another man only once.

ᚦᚦᚦ

Every religion says that in this world, man should keep doing good deeds because the good done to anyone in life does not go in vain; only God knows when it will come back to you in what form.

ᚦᚦᚦ

Every religion says that in this world, the living beings who support each other never see the situation, and the people who see the situation never support anyone.

ᑭᑭᑭ

Every religion says that if a man is not patient in this world, then he has neither present nor future.

ᑭᑭᑭ

Every religion says that in this world a man should remember that time is not dumb; it just remains silent, and only when the right time comes does it reveal that it also knows how to speak.

ᑭᑭᑭ

Every religion says that in this world, it may be difficult for a man to read the world in the form of a book, but the world is the teacher who teaches him everything.

ᑭᑭᑭ

Every religion says that if a person has more than what is needed in this world, he should share it with those who need it more.

ᑭᑭᑭ

Every religion says that it is the habit of every man in this world: if he does not get what he wants, then he does not have patience, and if he gets it, then he does not appreciate it.

ppp

Every religion says that every human being in this world has to understand that if his goal in his life is big then his struggle will also be equally big.

ppp

Every religion says that even if a man is illiterate in this world, if he learns to understand the feelings of any creature, then he is the most educated man in the world.

ppp

Every religion says that when a person is on the path of struggle in this world, he should not look back at that time, but after being successful, he should not forget to look back.

ppp

Every religion says that man in this world has to remember that you are good to other human beings as long as you fulfill their expectations, and all human beings are good to you as long as you are good to them. Don't have any hope.

ᐲᐲᐲ

Every religion says that the value of earthen pots and family in human life is known only to the maker, not the destroyer.

ᐲᐲᐲ

Every religion says that the definition of sin and virtue for human beings in this world is only that the act that hurts one's heart is sin, and the act that brings laughter to one's face is a virtue.

ᐲᐲᐲ

Every religion says that man should remember that problems in his life do not come to ruin him; they come only to identify the self-power within him.

ᐲᐲᐲ

Every religion says that man must fight for his rights in this world, but he should not be tempted by those over whom he has no rights.

ᐲᐲᐲ

Every religion says that in this world, a person who does not have knowledge of the right direction and right time sees even the rising sun setting.

ᛈᛈᛈ

Every religion says that where a man is not present in this world, his merits and demerits represent him.

ᛈᛈᛈ

Every religion says that in this world, a man should remember that no matter how proud the sea may be, it can drown the whole world, but a small drop of oil can cross that whole sea comfortably.

ᛈᛈᛈ

Every religion says that in this world, men will find lakhs of excuses to be scattered, but they themselves will have to find opportunities to join in their lives.

ᛈᛈᛈ

Every religion says that in this world God sends a man with such certainty. He doesn't have to bring anything when he is born, and he takes nothing with him when he is dead.

ᛈᛈᛈ

Every religion says that with the age of man in this world, his eyesight may become weak, but with time he starts seeing a lot clearer.

❧❧❧

Every religion says that no creature in this world should treat another creature in a way that it does not like for itself.

❧❧❧

Every religion says that in this world, men should remember that no matter how weak the mirror is, they are never afraid to show the truth.

❧❧❧

Every religion says that in this world, one should remember that the sweetness in a relationship starts from the moment when both parties see fewer qualities and more flaws in each other.

❧❧❧

Every religion says that if a person is fond of finding evil in this world, then it is better that he starts it with himself and not with others.

༒༒༒

Every religion says that there are only two personalities in man in this world, which enhance each other. The first when you have nothing is "endurance," and the second when you have everything is "behavior."

༒༒༒

Every religion says that in this world men should remember that time never stops and if yesterday was bad then today good will also come.

༒༒༒

Every religion says that in this world, men should keep the truth to themselves, love others, and have compassion for all; this is the grammar of life.

༒༒༒

Every religion says that in this world men should understand the power of words and that if they can make a relationship with someone then they can also ruin it.

༒༒༒

Every religion says that man should remember that hope and faith are never wrong in this world, but it depends on us for whom we hope and believe.

ᑭᑭᑭ

Every religion says that man should remember that the highest interest in this world comes from investing capital in knowledge. He should always try to write something that is worth reading or do something that is worth writing about.

ᑭᑭᑭ

Every religion says that in this world, a man should learn to trust God like a child, just as if he threw that child in the air, he would laugh and not fear. because he knows that the one who loves him will never let him fall.

ᑭᑭᑭ

Every religion says that good people have a specialty in human life; they are good even in bad times.

ᑭᑭᑭ

Every religion says that man should remember that even though there may be more than one heir to any man's property on earth, he himself is the heir to the deeds done by him.

ᠵᠵᠵ

Every religion says that man should remember that man's wealth is neither wealth nor property; it is his smiling family, good health, well-wishes, and his own contented mind.

ᠵᠵᠵ

Every religion says that one should always learn from life and that even silence does good deeds, as everyone must have seen trees that give shade to others.

ᠵᠵᠵ

Every religion says that one should remember to never show the power of their tongue to those who have taught them to speak.

ᠵᠵᠵ

Every religion says that if someone digs a pit in your path in this world, do not be upset, because these are the people from whose presence you will learn to jump.

ÞÞÞ

Every religion says that in human life in this world, meaning is very heavy because, after leaving, it lightens every relationship.

ÞÞÞ

Every religion says that if someone in this world asks why God is not visible, So to say, "Only God is there when no one is there for you."

ÞÞÞ

Every religion says that some human beings in this world often feel that the lives of others are better than their own, but while assessing this, they forget that there are also others for them.

ÞÞÞ

Every religion says that in this world, men should remember that ego is the opposite of knowledge; more knowledge, less ego.

ÞÞÞ

Every religion says that in this world, man should keep assessing himself from time to time to see whether his kindness, compassion, humanity, friendship, practicality, or humanity is decreasing or increasing.

ÞÞÞ

Every religion says that while making relationships in this world, it should be kept in mind that even though it is very easy to make relationships, it is very difficult to maintain them.

ÞÞÞ

Every religion says that in this world, one should remember that it is better to remain silent until one is fully aware of everything because incomplete truth is many times more dangerous than complete falsehood.

ÞÞÞ

Every religion says that in this world a person should remember that he cannot harm another person by being jealous of anyone, but he can definitely ruin his sleep and happiness.

ÞÞÞ

Every religion says that in this world a man should always understand that if he learns something from his mistakes, then those mistakes are like a ladder for him, but if he does not learn, then mistakes are like an ocean for him. The decision is yours, whether to climb or sink.

ﭒﭒﭒ

Every religion says that the day a man in this world will believe that everything is done according to the will of God, From that day onward, all his troubles will automatically end.

ﭒﭒﭒ

Every religion says that in this world, men should remember how right they are and how wrong they are in this life. Only two people know this: God and their conscience.

ﭒﭒﭒ

Every religion says that in this world, if a man has a complaint with anyone, he has to talk to him; if he has a complaint with most people, he has to talk to himself.

ﭒﭒﭒ

Every religion says that many times in the life of a man in this world, he gets out of the biggest troubles as if someone were supporting him, and the name of this invisible power is God.

ÞÞÞ

Every religion says that in this world, one should remember that no one rises suddenly; the sun also rises slowly and rises; the one who has the ability of patience and penance illuminates the world.

ÞÞÞ

Every religion says that in this world, men should remember that karma has neither paper nor book, yet the whole world is accounted for.

ÞÞÞ

They ask: "Is there really Ram Setu?" I said, "Oh, naive, the truth is that you are from Ram."

ÞÞÞ

Every religion says that human life is like a drop in this world, but the human ego is bigger than the ocean.

ÞÞÞ

Every religion says that in this world a man should remember that, just as no one can spoil iron but his own rust spoils it, similarly, man has no one else but his own bad thoughts that ruin him.

ppp

Every religion says that in this world, men should remember that they definitely get time to change their lives, but they do not get life again to change the time.

ppp

Every religion says that in this world, a man should always remain calm; only by remaining calm will he be able to strengthen his life because iron remains strong only when it is cold, not when it is hot.

ppp

Every religion says that if you feel happy in this world without any reason, then believe me, someone, somewhere, is praying to God for you.

ppp

Every religion says that it is almost impossible for a man to be empty in this world without bowing down, and if one wants to be free from ego, then bowing down is the only solution.

ᗊᗊᗊ

Every religion says that the wisest person in this world is the one who learns the most. The powerful one is the one who has control over his desires. A respected person is one who respects others. And rich is he who is happy with what is around him.

ᗊᗊᗊ

Every religion says that in this world man should purify his heart, not his intellect, to maintain relationships, that is, tell the truth, speak clearly, say it in front, if he is one, he will understand, and if he is a stranger, then he will be released.

ᗊᗊᗊ

Every religion says that all the human beings in this world have come into this world like a rough stone; the only difference is that someone was broken by their loved ones, and someone was carved by their loved ones.

ᗊᗊᗊ

Every religion says that in this world, men should remember that it is better to change the person in front of them than to take revenge.

ᐯᐯᐯ

Every religion says that in human life it is wise to praise from the heart, intervene with the mind, and react with discretion; otherwise, silence is better.

ᐯᐯᐯ

Every religion says that a man should remember that his prayers to God are never canceled; they are just accepted at the best of times.

ᐯᐯᐯ

Every religion says that man should make the most of the time he has; if a person keeps looking for good times, then his whole life will be reduced.

ᐯᐯᐯ

Every religion says that people in this world should forget the bitter thing and hold their hands, but people keep holding on to the matter and leaving their hands.

ᐯᐯᐯ

Every religion says that in this world, humans should remember that the person who walks on the path of struggle can change the world, and the one who has won the battle through the nights can emerge as the sun.

ᑭᑭᑭ

Every religion says that in human life, it is also necessary for every person to have some knowledge of chess because sometimes the front piece is moving and we keep on playing the relationship.

ᑭᑭᑭ

Every religion says that if human beings have to make their dreams come true in human life, then they have to change their paths, not their principles. because trees always change leaves, not roots.

ᑭᑭᑭ

Every religion says that in human life, humans should understand that God cannot be everywhere. That's why they made mothers, and mothers cannot be with us all the time.

ᑭᑭᑭ

Every religion says that in human life, humans should find their success not in the lines of the hands but in the sweat of the forehead.

ɲɲɲ

Every religion says that in human life, humans have to remember that no matter how many resources they have, it does not matter until they know how to use them.

ɲɲɲ

Every religion says that it is better in this world if humans keep their words in their minds and believe in doing more than speaking.

ɲɲɲ

Every religion says that if humans want to do something different in this world, they have to walk away from the crowd because the crowd gives courage but takes your identity from you.

ɲɲɲ

Every religion says that there are two best places in this world for human beings to live: in their hearts or in their prayers.

ɲɲɲ

Every religion says that human beings in this world should always remember that God is God without you, but you are nothing without God.

ᗽᗽᗽ

Every religion says that human beings in this world should always remember that nothing is available in this world without hard work, just as birds also have to come out of their nests for grain.

ᗽᗽᗽ

Every religion says that in this world, human beings need their nature like a lamp, which gives as much light in the palace of the emperor as in the hut of the poor.

ᗽᗽᗽ

Every religion says that human beings in this world should understand that matches burn themselves before burning anything else, similar to how someone who is angry destroys himself first and then others.

ᗽᗽᗽ

Every religion says that people in this world should remember that if they are not wrong, they should never present themselves to anyone, because the one who believes in them does not need an explanation, and the one who does not believe in them will not agree.

ÞÞÞ

Every religion says that people in this world should remember that an umbrella cannot stop the rain, but it definitely gives courage to stand in the rain. Similarly, self-confidence is not a measure of success, but it definitely gives you the motivation to struggle.

ÞÞÞ

Every religion says that in this world, humans should treat their relationships and money equally because both are difficult to earn but very easy to lose.

ÞÞÞ

Every religion says that in this world the peace of mind, good luck to be in control of the mind, bad luck to remember someone with the mind, and if someone remembers with the mind that is the ultimate good fortune.

ÞÞÞ

Every religion says that in the lives of human beings, only one member of their family is enough to settle or destroy their house.

ÞÞÞ

Every religion says that crematoriums in this world are full of the ashes of people who thought that the world could not go on without them.

ÞÞÞ

Every religion says that no man in this world is defeated when he falls; he is defeated when he refuses to rise after falling.

ÞÞÞ

Every religion says that the end of all human beings is the same in this world; what do humans do while they are alive? Only this thing makes a human being different from another human being.

ÞÞÞ

Every religion says that the only way to live with respect for all human beings in this world is to become the person they claim to be.

ÞÞÞ

Every religion says that power, money, hunger, greed, love, jealousy, ambition, or pride—everything that is more than what is needed in life—is poison for all human beings in this world.

ɓɓɓ

Every religion says that in this world, God resides in the houses where the parents laugh.

ɓɓɓ

Every religion says that in this world a man should forgive another man as you would expect from God for yourself.

ɓɓɓ

Every religion says that if there will never be a bad time in the life of a man in this world, then he will never be able to know about the bad people hidden in his life.

ɓɓɓ

Every religion says that in this world, humans should always remember that either they have to learn to change with the times, or they will have to learn to change the times because nothing will happen by cursing the compulsions. If a man wants to move forward, then he should learn to walk anyway in any situation.

☙☙☙

Every religion says that there is no use in spending the whole life in this world, no matter what other people say because in the end, those people will just say, "Ram Naam Satya Hai."

☙☙☙

Every religion says that in this world, human beings do not have to stay to collect flowers in their lives; move ahead, and flowers will continue to bloom on your path.

☙☙☙

Every religion says that human beings are wonderful in this world; when they like something, they don't see evil; when they hate something, they don't see good.

☙☙☙

Every religion says that the world is full of good people; if you are not meeting anyone, then become a good human first.

ᴘᴘᴘ

Every religion says that words are like a kind of food for human beings in this world. At what time, which word is to be served? The person who understands this is called a good cook.

ᴘᴘᴘ

It is good that Lord Shri Ram has taken the monkey army to Lanka. If he had taken humans, half of them would have been in favor of Ravana after seeing the golden Lanka.

ᴘᴘᴘ

Every religion says that in this world, men only know how much money they have; they never know how much time they have left. This is the biggest difference between money and time.

ᴘᴘᴘ

Every religion says that in this world a man cannot change the fate of anyone, even if he wants, but can show him the way by giving him good inspiration and, if given a chance, become someone's "charioteer," not "selfish."

ᴘᴘᴘ

Every religion says that in this world, humans should learn to smile because life teaches crying as soon as one is born.

❧❧❧

Every religion says that it does not matter to anyone in this world whether you exist or not. You will be treated as per your behavior and needs.

❧❧❧

Every religion says that in this world, man can learn from the Mahabharata that one's own understanding also matters; otherwise, Arjuna and Duryodhana's gurus were the same.

❧❧❧

Every religion says that human beings should not compare their lives with anyone else's in this world because both the sun and the moon shine, but at their own pace.

❧❧❧

Every religion says that people in this world should not waste their todays thinking that they have many tomorrows.

ϼϼϼ

Every religion says that in this world, human beings should understand that not every day can be good, but something good happens every day.

ϼϼϼ

Every religion says that in this world, human beings should understand that desires are only good, in which case there is no need to pledge self-respect.

ϼϼϼ

Every religion says that people in this world should understand that love is that string that is so strong that it can bind even God. But she does not bind herself to any bondage.

ϼϼϼ

Every religion says that in this world the support of loved ones is very necessary; if there is happiness, it increases, and if there is sorrow, it decreases.

ϼϼϼ

Every religion says that in this world humans should save only those memories that create a sparkle in their eyes! not those who cause wrinkles on the face.

ᐡᐡᐡ

Every religion says that life is a colorful book for everyone in this world; the only difference is that someone is reading every page by heart and someone is just turning pages.

ᐡᐡᐡ

Every religion says that even if one's parents are illiterate in this world, the ability to impart education and values is not found in any school in the world.

ᐡᐡᐡ

Every religion says that the whole game of life in this world is created by time and that man only plays his part.

ᐡᐡᐡ

Every religion says that half the beauty of human beings in this world is in their speech.

ᐡᐡᐡ

Every religion says that in this world, whether the ray of sun or hope in the lives of human beings, it removes all the darkness of life.

ᑀᑀᑀ

Every religion says that both anger and storms are equal in this world and that only after calming down can it be known how much damage has been done.

ᑀᑀᑀ

Every religion says that whatever is in a man's fate in this world will come by running away, but those who are not in luck will come and run away.

ᑀᑀᑀ

Every religion says that in this world, man's eyes only give him vision, but what he sees in others depends on his feelings.

ᑀᑀᑀ

Every religion says that in this world, humans should respect those who work and not those who fill their ears.

ᑀᑀᑀ

Every religion says that the one who loses in this world loses not from the world but from himself.

ÞÞÞ

Every religion says that in this world humans should be courageous because it is the path that will take them to their destination. Have you ever heard that darkness has not allowed dawn?

ÞÞÞ

Every religion says that evil in this world, big or small, always causes destruction because a small or big hole in the boat sinks the boat.

ÞÞÞ

Every religion says that the possibility of dreams coming true in this world is the thing that makes human life interesting.

ÞÞÞ

Every religion says that in this world in human life, I am the best; it is self-confidence, but I am the best; it is ego. And the ego is the cause of its destruction.

ÞÞÞ

Every religion says that the past in this world is not with man, but he has tomorrow to win.

❧❧❧

Every religion says that man must become great in this world, but not in front of the one who has made you great.

❧❧❧

Every religion says that in this world, when the medicine goes into the body instead of the pocket, only then is there an effect. In the same way, life is successful if good thoughts enter the heart, not just by listening.

❧❧❧

Every religion says that if a person dares to speak the truth in this world, then God will surely give him the power to face the consequences.

❧❧❧

Every religion says that in this world, self-respect comes with self-reliance in the life of man.

❧❧❧

Every religion says that God does not keep paper or books in this world, yet he keeps an account of the whole world.

ᕹᕹᕹ

Every religion says that in this world a man should remember that the greatest happiness in his life is in doing that work, which people say is not for him.

ᕹᕹᕹ

Every religion says that in this world, man can win by his virtues, not by his ego.

ᕹᕹᕹ

Every religion says that in this world, man gets everything, but only his mistake is not found.

ᕹᕹᕹ

Every religion says that human beings in this world should learn to ignore those who talk about them behind their backs, because they deserve to be in that place.

ᕹᕹᕹ

Every religion says that in this world, human beings should remember that if they do anything wrong in life, they cannot attain heaven because the doors of heaven do not open for those who do wrong deeds.

ᑭᑭᑭ

Every religion says that the problem in the Kali Yuga is not that the truth-tellers are decreasing; the problem is that the number of those who only listen to the truth of their own choosing has increased.

ᑭᑭᑭ

Every religion says that in the life of any human being in this world, if friends, books, paths, and thinking are wrong, they mislead, and if they are right, they make life.

ᑭᑭᑭ

Every religion says that in this world there is no heaven greater than happiness in the life of any human being and there is no hell other than despair.

ᑭᑭᑭ

Every religion says that all the human beings in this world are so poor that even their breath is not their own, and the rich are so great that they own the god who is ruling all the three worlds.

ᚦᚦᚦ

Every religion says that all human beings in this world should remember that the tree of the ego bears the fruit of destruction.

ᚦᚦᚦ

Every religion says that if the winds can change the course of the weather in human life, prayer can change the moments of trouble.

ᚦᚦᚦ

Every religion says that in this world, humans should remember that they have to put their strength in their thoughts, not in their voice, because the harvest is done by rain, not by flood.

ᚦᚦᚦ

Every religion says that ego is such a race in the life of every living being in this world where every winner loses.

ᚦᚦᚦ

Every religion says that in this world, human beings should not become good just for appearances because God knows them not from the outside but from the inside.

ᐳᐳᐳ

Every religion says that all human beings in this world have to write their own destiny because this is not a letter that can be written by others.

ᐳᐳᐳ

Every religion says that there is no disease in this world greater than fear and no medicine greater than courage.

ᐳᐳᐳ

Every religion says that in this world, the habit of sleeping for five minutes not only makes them sleep for hours, but this laziness life makes them many years behind.

ᐳᐳᐳ

Every religion says that in this world, those people are appreciated who deserve to be appreciated by others.

ᖚᖚᖚ

Every religion says that in this world suffering comes into the life of a human being so that he can understand the importance of happiness.

ᖚᖚᖚ

Every religion says that the basis of excellence in this world does not depend on sitting on a high seat but on high thinking.

ᖚᖚᖚ

Every religion says that in this world, human beings have to understand that if they have faith in their destiny, they will get what is written in it, and if they have faith in themselves, they will write whatever they want.

ᖚᖚᖚ

Every religion says that in this world, human beings do not need weather in order to do something in life; all the means will be gathered; they only need determination.

ᵱᵱᵱ

Every religion says that the habit of never giving up in this world can be transformed into the habit of winning every day.

ᵱᵱᵱ

Every religion says that in this world, humans should keep in mind that if their time is bad, they should work hard, and if their time is good, they should help someone.

ᵱᵱᵱ

Every religion says that in this world, God has sent all human beings like blank pages on earth, and on the basis of their qualities and qualifications, we have to fill them with our own worth.

ᵱᵱᵱ

Every religion says that it is not necessary to be great to start in this world, but to be great, a beginning is necessary.

ᵱᵱᵱ

Every religion says that a habit of time is very good in human life and that it changes.

ᕤᕤᕤ

Every religion says that in this world if a person keeps small things in his heart, then he will weaken his big relationships too.

ᕤᕤᕤ

Every religion says that no matter how wisely any person uses his words in this world, the listener understands and derives its meaning according to his ability and thoughts of the mind.

ᕤᕤᕤ

Every religion says that prayer full of faith made by any human in this world has the power to break all the shackles of darkness.

ᕤᕤᕤ

Every religion says that in this world a man should have the belief that he should not just let himself be defeated; if he succeeds in doing this, then no one can defeat him.

ᕤᕤᕤ

Every religion says that the secret of change in human life in this world is that you should not put all your energy into fighting the old but in creating the new.

ᐅᐅᐅ

Every religion says that in this world, if someone doubts your good deeds in human life, then it does not matter, because the doubt is always on the purity of gold, not on the soot of coal.

ᐅᐅᐅ

Every religion says that in this world, whether in defeat or victory, I am not afraid in the slightest, and whatever I get on the path of struggle, that is also right.

ᐅᐅᐅ

Every religion says that in this world, a person should remember that the one who is taking the test again and again will also give happiness when the time comes.

ᐅᐅᐅ

Every religion says that in this world two horses run in the mind of man, one of evil and the other of good; the one to whom man keeps on giving more food wins.

ᘖᘖᘖ

Every religion says that if anyone in this world does it for others, then there is no need to do it for yourself.

ᘖᘖᘖ

Every religion says that having a relationship in this world does not make a relationship, but keeping a relationship builds a relationship.

ᘖᘖᘖ

Every religion says that it is not easy for human beings to find happiness within themselves in this world, and it is not possible to find it anywhere else.

ᘖᘖᘖ

Every religion says that you should save your mind from becoming Kaikeyi (a character in RAMAYANA) in this world because when the mind becomes Kaikeyi, some mantra (aa character in RAMAYANA) is definitely available to fill the ear.

ᘖᘖᘖ

Every religion says that in this world, man can make medicine for every disease of his body, but until he makes medicine for the bitterness of his tongue, his problems will not end.

ᗖᗖᗖ

Every religion says that in this world, a lamp of "soil" fights with the darkness all night; you are a lamp of "God"; what are you afraid of?

ᗖᗖᗖ

Every religion says that you shouldn't stay in this world only with those who make you happy; spend some time also with those who are happy to see you.

ᗖᗖᗖ

Every religion says that in this world "roof" should not be proud of being "roof" because as soon as one more floor is built on it, "roof" will become "floor."

ᗖᗖᗖ

Every religion says that in this world, some men fear that God is watching, and some believe that God is watching.

ᗖᗖᗖ

Every religion says that in this world, birds never build nests for the future of their children; they just teach them the art of flying.

ㅂㅂㅂ

Every religion says that tolerance in this world is not a sign of weakness but a sign of strength, just as Lord Shri Ram gave proof of his strength by pleading with the ocean for three days.

ㅂㅂㅂ

Every religion says that in this world, man can fight with the world but not with his loved ones, because to live with his loved ones is not to win.

ㅂㅂㅂ

Every religion says that what are the words in this world? If the smell is attached, and if it is lost, then the wound.

ㅂㅂㅂ

Every religion says that in this world it takes a minute to make fun of relationships, but we forget that life is decorated with relationships.

🙏🙏🙏

Every religion says that in this world, God creates everyone from the same soil; the only difference is that someone is beautiful from "outside" and someone from "inside."

🙏🙏🙏

Every religion says that there is a difference in the feet walking in this world, one in front and one behind, but neither the one ahead is proud nor the one behind is insulted because they know that after some time this situation is about to change in me; this is called life.

🙏🙏🙏

Every religion says that when time judges in human life, witnesses are not needed.

🙏🙏🙏

Every religion says that when human beings earn money in this world, things come into the house, but when they earn someone's blessings, with wealth comes happiness, health, and love.

🙏🙏🙏

Every religion says that no matter how much praise is given in this world, insults should be done very carefully because insult is a debt, which everyone pays with interest when given the opportunity.

ᗧᗧᗧ

Every religion says that man is a misguided deity in this world; if he can walk in the right direction, no one is better than him.

ᗧᗧᗧ

Every religion says that even storms are defeated in this world where the boats are stubborn.

ᗧᗧᗧ

Every religion says that the best sight in this world is the one who can see his shortcomings, because you wake up externally every day from your sleep, but if you wake up internally, that's a rare scenario.

ᗧᗧᗧ

Every religion says that in this world, if the stitching of relationships is done by feelings, then it is difficult to break, and if it is done by selfishness, then it is difficult to survive.

ᗧᗧᗧ

Every religion says that people in this world should listen to the advice of everyone, but should only do that for which their courage and conscience allow.

ৡৡৡ

Every religion says that if human beings have to move ahead in life in this world, then ego, greed, anger, and fear have to be thrown in the dustbin.

ৡৡৡ

Every religion says that in this world, if a person learns to remain calm in life, then he will find himself very strong, because iron remains strong only when it is cold, but it can be molded into any shape when it is hot.

ৡৡৡ

Every religion says that ego is the root cause of all the big mistakes in the life of a man in this world.

ৡৡৡ

Every religion says that in this world, all human beings are faster than their speed, but no one has been able to get ahead of their time and luck.

ᛈᛈᛈ

Every religion says that in this world, education and rites are the basic mantras of living life; education will never let you down, and culture will never let you fall.

ᛈᛈᛈ

Every religion says that in human life the praise given by the opponent is the best fame.

ᛈᛈᛈ

Every religion says that it is our good fortune to have good people in this world, and it is our ability to take care of them.

ᛈᛈᛈ

Every religion says that in this world, humans should keep their hearts like the ocean; only then will the rivers come to meet themselves.

ᛈᛈᛈ

Every religion says that in this world, the person who has beautiful thoughts in his mind finds the whole world beautiful.

ᐅᐅᐅ

Every religion says that in this world if a man sets a time limit for dreams, then that becomes his goal.

ᐅᐅᐅ

Every religion says that if human beings have the courage to accept and the determination to improve in this world, they can learn a lot.

ᐅᐅᐅ

Every religion says that no human life is easy in this world, but he can make it easier, some with style and some by ignorance.

ᐅᐅᐅ

Every religion says that the most profitable deal for any human being in this world is to sit with the elders because, in a few moments, they give you years of experience.

ᐅᐅᐅ

Every religion says that the lucky ones in this world are those who get "time" and "understanding" together, because often "time" does not have "understanding," and when "understanding" comes, "time" gets out of hand.

ÞÞÞ

Every religion says that if you keep on laughing in this world, then the world is with you; otherwise, tears do not even find a place in your eyes.

ÞÞÞ

Every religion says that the struggle in the lives of all human beings in this world is the invitation of nature, and the one who accepts it moves forward.

ÞÞÞ

Every religion says that there is only one heart in this world, which works without rest, so keep it happy, whether it is yours or your loved ones'.

ÞÞÞ

Every religion says that in this world do not get entangled in the search whether there is a God or not; keep the search whether we ourselves are humans or not.

ÞÞÞ

Every religion says that seven generations experience what is fortunately received in this world. Seven generations suffer the fruits of dishonesty.

ⵒⵒⵒ

Every religion says that only hope in human life is such an energy that any darkness of life can be illuminated.

ⵒⵒⵒ

Every religion says that in human life time is the only king, a person just acts like a king.

ⵒⵒⵒ

Every religion says that in this world, humans should learn to speak sweetly, to bow down, and to be most loving.

ⵒⵒⵒ

Every religion says that pride does not belong to anyone in this world; even before breaking, the piggy bank feels that all the money belongs to him.

ⵒⵒⵒ

Every religion says that if a snake is seen at home in this world, then people beat it with sticks, and if it is seen on Shivling, then they give milk. People respect your position and place, not you.

ᐅᐅᐅ

Every religion says that power and money are the fruits of life in this world and that family and friends are the root of life.

ᐅᐅᐅ

Every religion says that in this world, people should remember that what can be given from the heart is not given with the hands.

ᐅᐅᐅ

Every religion says that in this world, any human being should be the reason for someone's smile or not, but he should never be the reason for anyone's pain.

ᐅᐅᐅ

Every religion says that the name and identity of any human being in this world may be small, but it should be enough in itself.

ᐅᐅᐅ

Every religion says that this is why it happens in this world that people leave relationships but do not give up stubbornness.

ϷϷϷ

Every religion says that the tongue of any human being never slips in this world; always remember. Whatever is going on in the brain, it comes out on the tongue.

ϷϷϷ

Every religion says that if human beings want wonderful relationships in this world, they must follow them deeply; wonderful pearls are never found on the shore.

ϷϷϷ

Every religion says that in this world people run away from the mud so that the clothes do not get spoiled, and that is why the mud gets the false pride that people are afraid of it.

ϷϷϷ

Every religion says that there are many deals in the lives of human beings in this world, but those who sell happiness and those who buy sorrow are not found.

ϷϷϷ

Every religion says that trust is important in this world, but don't sit on anyone's trust.

ϷϷϷ

Every religion says that the bad news for human beings in this world is that time flies, and the good news is that you are its driver.

ϷϷϷ

Every religion says that it is good for human beings to be beautiful in this world, but it is more beautiful to be good.

ϷϷϷ

Every religion says that in the journey of human life in this world, it often happens that the difficult decision is better.

ϷϷϷ

Every religion says that the life of human beings is very short in this world; live it with laughter as much as possible because memories, not time, come back.

ÞÞÞ

Every religion says that the distance between possible and impossible in this world depends on the determination of the person.

ÞÞÞ

Every religion says that in this world, human beings get excuses by thinking about the problem; thinking about the solution gives way.

ÞÞÞ

Every religion says that in this world the person who is never familiar with the struggle, history is a witness for those kinds of people, and they never get famous.

ÞÞÞ

Every religion says that in this world, men should always try to avoid making small mistakes because they stumble not on mountains but on stones.

ÞÞÞ

Every religion says that in this world, what is in the mind of man should be clearly stated because in this world, decisions are made by telling the truth, and by telling lies, there are distances.

ᐳᐳᐳ

Every religion says that some human beings have this ability in this world, and no matter how much good you say, they will find evil in it, so take care of yourself.

ᐳᐳᐳ

Every religion says that hope never leaves anyone in this world; only people leave it in a hurry.

ᐳᐳᐳ

Every religion says that in this world the crowd always walks on the path, which seems easy, but it does not mean that the crowd always walks on the right path. Choose your own path, because no one knows you better than you.

ᐳᐳᐳ

Every religion says that as long as we keep helping each other in this world, no one will fall, whether it is in business, family, or society.

ᑀᑀᑀ

Every religion says that all human beings in this world need to create a storm of their deeds, more than beating their heads against the door of fate, because only by doing this will the doors of fate open.

ᑀᑀᑀ

Every religion says that in this world, the world is won by words and mind; even today, the heart is won by the heart itself.

ᑀᑀᑀ

Every religion says that the luckiest person in this world is the one who equates hunger with food, sleep with a bed, and religion with wealth.

ᑀᑀᑀ

Every religion says that when a person's mind is weak in human life, then his circumstances become a problem. When the mind is stable, situations become challenges, and when the mind is strong, circumstances become opportunities.

ᑀᑀᑀ

Every religion says that in this world a person should always keep the effect of a lamp, that too without seeing whose house was illuminated by it.

ԿԿԿ

Every religion says that in this world, a person's care for another human being shows how much he cares for another person. Otherwise, there are no scales to measure relationships.

ԿԿԿ

Every religion says that everyone needs respect in this world, but people forget to give it.

ԿԿԿ

Every religion says that if you have to ask something from God in this world, then always pray for the fulfillment of your mother's dreams, and you yourself will touch the heights of the sky.

ԿԿԿ

Every religion says that in this world, someone is enough, and someone alone is enough.

ԿԿԿ

Every religion says that in this world, man should have faith in both God and time in his bad times because time turns coal into diamond and the Lord ranks as king.

ᕽᕽᕽ

Every religion says that in this world, a person should accept what he feels is good and give up what he feels is bad. be it thought, deed, or man.

ᕽᕽᕽ

Every religion says that in this world, man should be identified not with big people but with those who support him on time.

ᕽᕽᕽ

Every religion says that in this world a man should remember that when he is climbing the stairs of the heights, he should behave very well with the people left behind because, while descending, the same people will meet him again on the way.

ᕽᕽᕽ

Every religion says that in this world there are bigger parents than God because God gives both happiness and sorrow, but parents give only happiness.

༄༄༄

Every religion says that if gifts are not given to a child by a man in this world, he will cry for a while, and if the sacraments are not given, he will cry for the rest of his life.

༄༄༄

Every religion says that who should keep an account in this world, how much was given to whom, and who saved how much, so God applied simple mathematics and sent everyone empty-handed and called them empty-handed.

༄༄༄

Every religion says that in this world a wise man finds a way in his difficult time and a weak person pretends.

༄༄༄

Every religion says that the most difficult posture in this world is "assurance," the longest breath is "faith," the most difficult yoga is "disconnection," and the best yoga is "cooperation."

☙☙☙

Every religion says that in this world, a person's "getting down in your mind" and "getting out of your mind" depend only on their behavior.

☙☙☙

Every religion says that man is a shop in this world, and the tongue is its lock; once the lock opens up, only then is it known whether the shop is made of gold or of coal.

☙☙☙

Every religion says that there is nothing better for him in human life in this world than his today, because his tomorrow will never come and today will never go.

☙☙☙

Every religion says that in this world, a person does not know how many days he has to stay in the shelter of the world; that is why he should win everyone's hearts; this is the jewel of life.

☙☙☙

Every religion says that in human life, after one of a person's dreams is shattered, he must see his second dream with courage; this courage is called life.

ᛈᛈᛈ

Every religion says that in this world, man should not compare his life with anyone. Just like there is no comparison between the "Sun" and "Moon," they shine as per their defined timings.

ᛈᛈᛈ

Every religion says that in this world the wounds of a man's mouth heal the fastest, but the wounds of words spoken with the mouth heal the longest.

ᛈᛈᛈ

Every religion says that in this world, those who have to be their own, they themselves become their own; they are not made their own by telling anyone else.

ᛈᛈᛈ

Every religion says that one has to go far in this world just to know who is near.

ᛈᛈᛈ

Every religion says that in this world, the better the speech and thoughts of a man, the more success he will get.

ᏢᏢᏢ

Every religion says that in this world, the people who are not able to beat you "by running" in the race of life try to defeat you "by breaking."

ᏢᏢᏢ

Every religion says that in this world it is not wrong to bow down in relationships in human life because, if seen, even the sun sets for the moon.

ᏢᏢᏢ

Every religion says that no one can close the path God has opened for you in this world.

ᏢᏢᏢ

Every religion says that the silence of a person in this world is not his weakness but his nobleness; otherwise, he who knows how to bear it also knows how to say it.

ᏢᏢᏢ

Every religion says that no human being in this world is full of all qualities, so some shortcomings should be ignored and relationships should be maintained.

ⵉⵉⵉ

Every religion says that there is no fixed definition of earning for human beings in this world because experience, relationships, respect, and good friends are all forms of earning.

ⵉⵉⵉ

Every religion says that it is not a big deal for humans to earn bread in this world, but it is a big thing to eat bread with family.

ⵉⵉⵉ

Every religion says that in this world, humans should keep the door of their house small, because the one who has bowed down thinks that he is his own.

ⵉⵉⵉ

Every religion says that in this world people leave you at the slightest thing and that God holds you with a little prayer.

ᐔᐔᐔ

Every religion says that in this world, men should remember that time changes all the time. Just give it some time.

ᐔᐔᐔ

Every religion says that it is better for human beings to try once in their lives than to regret later.

ᐔᐔᐔ

Every religion says that if human beings face difficulties in this world, then they should be avoided by saying, "Just tell the destination, though I have not reached it yet, since there are difficulties, but remember I haven't stopped yet."

ᐔᐔᐔ

Every religion says that in this world, human beings should keep knocking on the doors of each other's minds so that, even if the meetings do not sound right, they will keep on coming.

ᐔᐔᐔ

Every religion says that in this world, a person learns to speak after 2 years of birth. But it takes a whole lifetime to learn how to speak.

❦❦❦

Every religion says that time, faith, and respect are such rare birds in this world! Those who fly away do not come back.

❦❦❦

Every religion says that all human beings in this world dream in their sleep, but God wakes them up every day and gives them a chance to fulfill those dreams. That is why we should give thanks to God every day.

❦❦❦

Every religion says that in this world, people should always remember that faith and honesty are the invaluable heritage of human beings.

❦❦❦

Every religion says that when a person gets into trouble in this world, then he starts seeing Griha Dosha, Vastu Dosha, Pitra Dosha, Shani Dosha, and

Kaal Sarp Dosh; only his own fault is not visible.

ppp

Every religion says that if you have happiness in your heart while helping others in this world, then that is service; everything else pretends.

ppp

Every religion says that in this world, man is created by his beliefs; as he thinks, so he is.

ppp

Every religion says that talent is of no importance in this world without willpower.

ppp

Every religion says that no man in this world can see evil in attachment, and he cannot see good in hatred.

ppp

Every religion says that one who has hope in this world does not lose even after losing.

ppp

Every religion says that in this world, through which "doubt" enters the lives of human beings, "love" and "faith" go out through the same door.

❧❧❧

Every religion says that the value of human beings in this world is in what they are, not what they have.

❧❧❧

Every religion says that bad company for a human being in this world is like coal, which burns hands when it is hot and turns hands black when it is cold.

❧❧❧

Every religion says that every person in this world is better than any other person in some way or another, and we should learn those things from him.

❧❧❧

Every religion says that the only ones who win in this world are those who hold on to hope in every situation.

❧❧❧

Every religion says that if a man wants to be successful in this world, he should always keep in mind that he should not rely on strangers because you have to walk on your own two feet.

❧❧❧

Every religion says that in this world, if you keep doing good like flowing water, evil will itself be washed away like garbage.

❧❧❧

Every religion says that the greatest use of life in this world is to invest it in something that will remain hereafter.

❧❧❧

Every religion says that in this world, along with fasting food, greed, greed, slander, lust, anger, and bad thoughts should also be there.

❧❧❧

Every religion says that when you carve yourself out in this world, then the world searches for you.

❧❧❧

Every religion says that in this world, men should keep relationships like sandalwood so that even if the pieces are a thousand, the fragrance does not go away.

ÞÞÞ

Every religion says that in this world, men should keep in mind that nothing will happen by just looking at the clock; they will have to do what the clock does and keep going continuously.

ÞÞÞ

Every religion says that there can be no better friend in this world than God.

ÞÞÞ

Every religion says that if a man in this world decides with his heart what he has to do, then his mind will automatically devise ideas.

ÞÞÞ

Every religion says that there are only two things in this world: a smile and a prayer, and the more you distribute them, the more you will get.

ÞÞÞ

Every religion says that as long as a man lives with his fear in this world, he will not be able to live his dreams.

ÞÞÞ

Every religion says that in this world, one's simple nature is not his weakness, but the sanskars given by his parents.

ÞÞÞ

Every religion says that if someone is the most powerful in this world, then it is willpower. You can get everything in the world through this. If you want, you will find the way automatically.

ÞÞÞ

Every religion says that the time is the same for every human being in this world, and if he wants to make gold in that time, he should either waste it by sleeping.

ÞÞÞ

Gave a wonderful taunt in the temple today. God said, "You only come to ask; come to meet me sometime."

❧❧❧

Every religion says that when the games of childhood are over in human life, then the games of luck start.

❧❧❧

Every religion says that in this world, a man should remember that his life can suddenly take a good turn from anywhere in his life, which is why he should never be disappointed.

❧❧❧

Every religion says that in this world it is not necessary to know your age; it is important to know what age you think.

❧❧❧

Every religion says that in this world you should offer yourself to God, this is the best support. He who knows its support is always free from fear, worry and grief.

❧❧❧

Every religion says that in this world fragrance is found automatically to those who cultivate flowers.

ꕔꕔꕔ

Every religion says that compare yourself with a quiet and humble person in this world, you will feel that your pride is definitely worth giving up.

ꕔꕔꕔ

Every religion says that in this world a man should remember that he has to make as much effort to become a noble person as he does to become beautiful.

ꕔꕔꕔ

Every religion says that in this world small thoughts are capable of bringing big changes in the life of man. Just like the door is smaller than the house, the lock is smaller than the door, the key is smaller than the lock... but a small key opens the whole house.

ꕔꕔꕔ

Every religion says that in this world a teacher is necessary in the life of a man, not the ego.

ꕔꕔꕔ

Every religion says that in this world, the eyes also have to be opened for light; the darkness does not go away just because the sun comes out.

ᐇᐇᐇ

Every religion says that in this world, you will always hear from the mouths of successful people that, "If the sunshine on the path to success was not there, then we would have fallen asleep."

ᐇᐇᐇ

Every religion says that if a man starts giving in this world, these things will start coming in his life, respect as well as wealth.

ᐇᐇᐇ

Every religion says that if you want only a handful in this world then become Alexander, if you want the whole universe then become Kabir.

ᐇᐇᐇ

Every religion says that in this world, the creation of god seems differently to everyone, according to their vision.

ᐇᐇᐇ

Every religion says that in this world, human beings feet take them to the temple and their conduct take them to God.

ϷϷϷ

Every religion says that in this world, the fruit of hard work and the solution to the problem are definitely available at the right time.

ϷϷϷ

Every religion says that the "strength" of a person in this world can be estimated, but not his "spirit."

ϷϷϷ

Every religion says that only love has the power to bow someone down in this world; otherwise, what was the need for Ramji to eat the berries tasted by Shabri?

ϷϷϷ

Every religion says that your goal in this world should be right because even termites work day and night, but they do not create but destroy.

ϷϷϷ

Every religion says that you should always remember in this world that there is no destination to which there is no way to get.

ÞÞÞ

Every religion says that the fire of revenge in this world burns others less and more itself, which is why the idea of not taking revenge on anyone but changing oneself is better.

ÞÞÞ

Every religion says that in this world a person should always keep his words sweet so that even if he has to take them back, he does not feel bitter.

ÞÞÞ

Every religion says that a man should never blame his luck in this world because he has been born as a human being; if this is not luck, then what else is?

ÞÞÞ

Every religion says that it is not possible to achieve anything in this world without renunciation, because even to breathe, one has to exhale first.

ÞÞÞ

Every religion says that a sweet tongue, good habits, good behavior, and good people are always respected in this world.

ƥƥƥ

Every religion says that if your voice is high in this world, only a few people will listen, but if the talk is high, then many people will listen.

ƥƥƥ

Every religion says that in this world, humans should give time to every relationship in their lives. Do you know that tomorrow we will have time and there will be no relationship?

ƥƥƥ

Every religion says that for longevity in this world, one should halve the sorrow, drink twice as much water, exercise three times, laugh four times, and meditate on God 100 times.

ƥƥƥ

Every religion says that in this world even a soil lamp fights with the darkness all night; then you are a gift from God; what are you afraid of?

Every religion says that when man is filled with anger in this world, then it's hell for him, and when he is filled with compassion, then it's heaven.

Every religion says that if hard work becomes a habit in this world, then success becomes luck.

Every religion says that this is the principle of successful relationships in this world: forget all those things that are meaningless.

Every religion says that in this world, man's mistake is that he forgets God.

Every religion says that the best cure for man's anxiety in this world is his trust in God.

❧❧❧

Every religion says that in this world, if the relationship is in the heart, then it is not broken even by breaking, and if it is in the mind, then it is not connected even by connecting.

❧❧❧

Every religion says that in this world, if the relationship is in the heart, then it is not broken even by breaking, and if it is in the mind, then it is not connected even by connecting.

❧❧❧

Every religion says that human life in this world is like a guitar, and if a person learns to play it properly, then there is joy in his life.

❧❧❧

Every religion says that happiness in this world is medicine, which is not found in any part of the world but only within itself.

❧❧❧

Every religion says that whenever the boat of human life gets stuck in the middle of this world, only the boat called God crosses it.

ᭂᭂᭂ

Every religion says that in this world, you should become rich with your mind and not with money, because even if there are golden urns in the temple, one has to bow down on the steps of the temple.

ᭂᭂᭂ

Every religion says that in this world it is very important for man to bow down from his mind; only by bowing his head does one get the blessings of God.

ᭂᭂᭂ

Every religion says that to change life in this world, one has to fight; to make it easy, one has to understand.

ᭂᭂᭂ

Every religion says that in this world the king in the country, the teacher in the society, and the father in the family are never ordinary; both creation and destruction are in their hands.

ᚦᚦᚦ

Every religion says that in this world, a person can be arbitrary in doing his deeds but not in his karma.

ᚦᚦᚦ

Every religion says that to be successful in this world, the desire for success should be greater than the fear of failure.

ᚦᚦᚦ

Every religion says that the one who suffers sorrow in this world can be happy later, but the one who gives sorrow can never be happy.

ᚦᚦᚦ

Every religion says that not everyone can become great in this world, but everyone can be better than where they are at the moment.

ᚦᚦᚦ

Every religion says that in this world, man cannot see evil in attachment or good in hatred.

ᚦᚦᚦ

Every religion says that if there is a desire for peace in this world, then first pacify the desire.

ᗥᗥᗥ

Every religion says that in this world a man should not indulge in unaccounted-for laughs, but he should take care of what he has got.

ᗥᗥᗥ

Every religion says that it is always beneficial for a person to wake up early in this world, whether it is from sleep, ego, or fear.

ᗥᗥᗥ

Every religion says that this often happens in connection with misunderstandings in this world; every brick thinks that the wall rests on it.

ᗥᗥᗥ

Every religion says to keep helping people in this world because, according to a principle of nature, the well from which people keep drinking water never dries up.

ᗥᗥᗥ

Every religion says that due to the arrogance of man in this world, all three—wealth, glory, and lineage—are lost. If you don't believe, then see Ravana, the Kauravas, and Kansa.

Every religion says that life in this world is not what we get; it is what we make.

Every religion says that to make mistakes in this world is "nature," to believe is "culture," and to improve is "progress."

Every religion says that scissors should not be used on the thread whose knots can be opened in this world.

Every religion says that in this world, a person remembers all the things that are forgotten, and that is why there is controversy in his life.

Every religion says that in this world, believe that there is no giant like a Banyan or a Peepal. But remember that even the basil growing in pots is no less than anyone.

ᗠᗠᗠ

Every religion says that many people in this world have come up after recovering from sorrows in life. What is falling apart can rise again; just have courage. When sorrow comes into our lives, our patience is tested.

ᗠᗠᗠ

Every religion says that only money can buy happiness in this world. There are many people who have a lot of money but not much happiness.